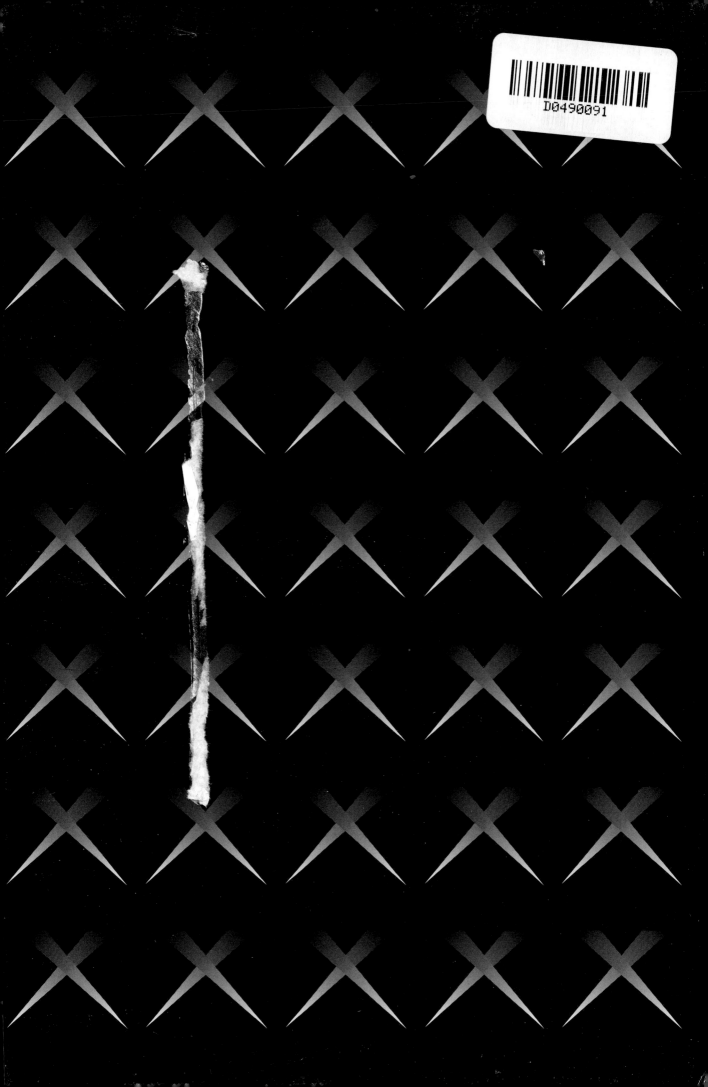

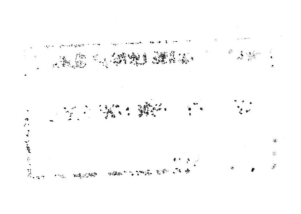

BLITZ

CAXTON EDITIONS
AN IMPRINT OF CAXTON PUBLISHING GROUP
20 BLOOMSBURY STREET, LONDON WC1 3QA

ISBN 1 84067 159 9

A COPY OF THE CIP DATA IS AVAILABLE FROM THE
BRITISH LIBRARY UPON REQUEST.

DESIGNED AND PRODUCED FOR CAXTON EDITIONS
BY KEITH POINTING DESIGN CONSULTANCY

REPROGRAPHICS BY GA GRAPHICS
PRINTED AND BOUND IN
SINGAPORE BY APP PRINTING

ACKNOWLEDGMENTS
THE IMPERIAL WAR MUSEUM
CHISLEHURST CAVES
DESIGN AND PRODUCTION ASSISTANCE:
MIKI HIRAI AND RIKAKO SUZUKI
COPY EDITOR ROSANNA NEGROTTI

BLITZ

A PICTORIAL HISTORY

TEXT BY

DR CORINNA PENISTON-BIRD

CAXTON EDITIONS

CONTENTS

INTRODUCTION

In 1958, A YOUNG WOMAN was happily walking down a sunny street in a French village. The next moment, she found herself cowering under a shop counter surrounded by astounded villagers. My mother had reacted instinctively to a siren. It belonged to the local fire engine, but sounded exactly like the ululating wail of the air-raid siren with which she had grown up as a small child in wartime Lincolnshire. The instinct to seek cover remained embedded thirteen years after the conclusion of the war.

LEFT: Alice Taylor, aged 81, points out to a policeman the 'bruises' to her Anderson shelter in which she and seven of her family were saved when a bomb partly demolished her house in a London district on 28 July 1941.
PREVIOUS PAGE: London firefighters tackle a blaze.

For many Britons who remained in the United Kingdom in the Second World War, the experience of the Blitz remains one of the dominant memories of the war. The term 'Blitz' stems from the German *Blitzkrieg*, or 'lightning war', a description used in the world press to describe the rapidity of the German conquests on mainland Europe between September 1939 and June 1940. With its connotations of danger from the air, it became the popular term for the German aerial bombardment. Although 'the Blitz' is often used to refer to the bombing of London between 1940 and 1941, this collection includes images from air raids throughout the war and across the United Kingdom, serving as a reminder that London was only one of the many targeted areas.

RIGHT: British soldiers practising wearing gas masks before the war.

OVERLEAF: Air-raid damage from the First World War. Wellington Street in London was damaged in an Airship raid on 13-14 October 1915.

The Blitz was not the first experience of air warfare on the British mainland. Bombing raids in the First World War had left a profound impression on policy-makers and the general public alike. In 1917-18, the Germans had staged 103 raids (51 by airship) dropping three hundred tons of bombs, mainly on London. These raids resulted in 1,413 casualties and public outrage. The Government concluded that, in Stanley Baldwin's famous words of 1932, the bomber would always get through. Based on these attacks, it was predicted future air raids would cost up to 3,000 lives and result in 12,000 wounded per attack, creating colossal damage and destroying public morale. The bombing of Guernica, the Spanish town attacked by the Condor Legion on 27 April 1937, provided further evidence that in any future war civilians would be targeted with explosive and incendiary bombs. It was also assumed that the gas attacks experienced in the trenches on the Western Front

OVERLEAF: Coventry Cathedral after it was destroyed.

would be repeated from the air. Pillar boxes were therefore given a rim of gas-sensitive yellow paint to offer warning of toxic levels in the air, and the nation was supplied with gas masks. Masks were also designed to protect babies in prams, as well as carthorses and pet dogs. Although it was illegal for individuals not to carry them, the masks were never needed. The main legacy of the fear of gas was in terminology. The end of an air raid was popularly labelled not 'raiders passing', but the 'all clear', a term intended to indicate that gas had been successfully cleared after an attack.

Although these predictions as to the scale and nature of air warfare proved too pessimistic, the air raids of the Second World War did bring the war home to the British public on a scale never experienced previously. This collection is intended to convey some of the flavour of those experiences and to offer a visual record of the bombing of the United Kingdom.

CHAPTER 1

THE PHASES AND WEAPONS OF THE BLITZ

THE DECLARATION OF WAR on 3 September 1939 was accompanied by the first air-raid warning in London, triggered by a single French aeroplane arriving off schedule. It was to be the first of many such alerts. Initially, the German air campaign was aimed at the destruction of the RAF and its bases. However, even when military targets were the objective, the range of targets included docks and railway stations, which meant that civilian casualties quickly began to mount. Among the first

LEFT: Air raid on Manchester, 23 November 1940.

victims were the poisonous snakes of London Zoo, which had to be destroyed in case they escaped in a raid. (The treasures of the National Gallery had better luck: they were evacuated to a cave in a disused slate quarry in North Wales.) The first civilian casualty was Jim Imbister, killed in an air raid on the Orkney Islands in April 1940. London was first bombed accidentally on 24 August 1940 and the bombing of civilian targets escalated from there.

The Blitz went in phases. The first fell between 9 September 1940 and May 1941, the period which included the London Blitz. In the autumn of 1940, the capital was raided for seventy-six consecutive nights, with

OVERLEAF: 14 October 1940. When bombs fell in London during the days of the big raids, one of them made this crater in a Balham street, breaking the mains, twisting tramlines and partly engulfing a bus.

Double-decker tram destroyed in London as a firestorm rages in the background.

only one exception. By the end of the war, the chance of being killed in an air attack was one in 160 for Londoners, and one in 800 for citizens elsewhere. The way in which Londoners met the Blitz, at least as represented in the media, therefore became the paradigm for other areas to emulate.

The second phase began with the bombing of Coventry in November 1940, adding the new word 'coventration' to wartime vocabulary. Not only was one third of the city rendered uninhabitable, but 554 people were killed and 865 wounded: nearly all inhabitants knew somebody who had been killed, injured or made homeless.

OVERLEAF LEFT: A gas rattle, intended to be used to alert the public in case of a gas attack.

OVERLEAF RIGHT: A warden wearing his respirator ready with a stirrup pump.

Even when the Luftwaffe became more embroiled on the Eastern Front, British territory was still targeted in small-scale 'Tip-and-Run' attacks, mainly on coastal areas such as Tyneside, Great Yarmouth and Lowestoft. These were intended to sap morale and prove that the war against Britain would continue.

On 14 April 1942, the RAF bombed the historic city of Lübeck. Hitler ordered that air warfare against Britain was to become more aggressive, with preference being given to areas where 'attacks are likely to have the greatest possible effect on civilian life.' These 'terror attacks' were carried out in the Baedeker Raids between 23 April and 6 June. The historic cities targeted included Exeter, Bath, Norwich, York and Canterbury. Nearly one-and-a-half thousand people were killed.

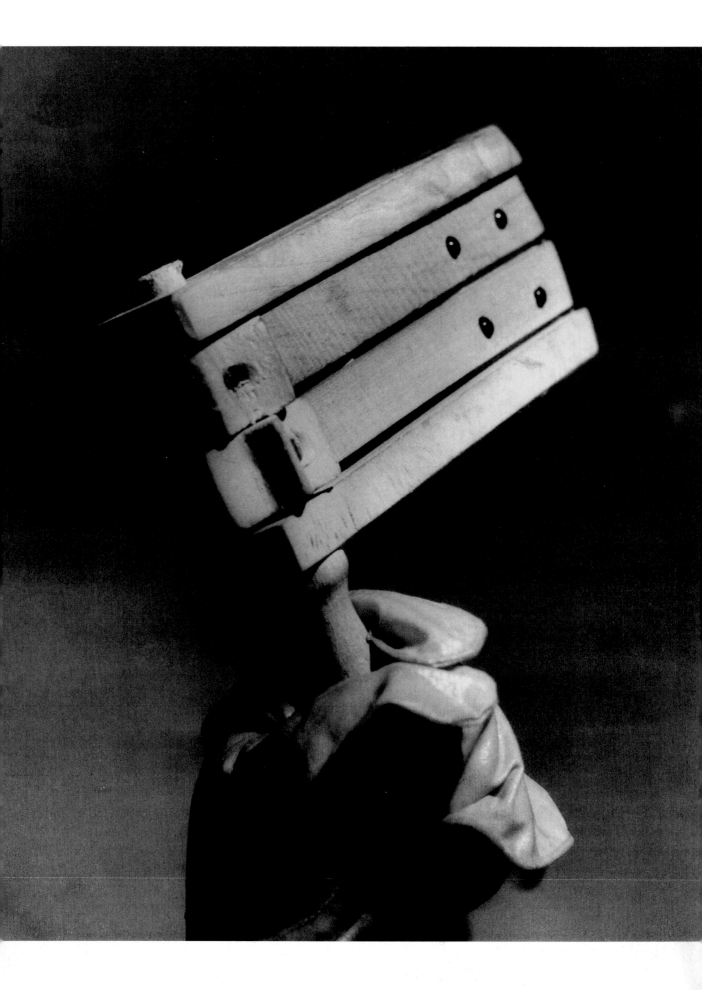

LEFT: RAF bomber attacks a flying-bomb depot at Trossy St Maximin, situated north of Paris, close to the river Oise. The depot consisted of a number of quarries on the sides of which were tunnels. This photograph, taken by an aircraft which took part in the attack on 3 August 1944, shows one Lancaster bomber over the target from which great clouds of smoke are rising.

OVERLEAF: The Thames during the first mass air raid on London, 7 September 1940. The bombers came over in the late afternoon and after a short pause continued throughout the night. In the foreground, a river tug plies its trade against the background of Tower Bridge and fierce fires rage in the dock area.

The fourth and final phase of the Blitz began in June 1944, when the V1s and V2s were launched at the South East and London. In 1945, following the successful Allied advances on the continent, the air attacks on Britain came to end: the last raid on Kent by the Luftwaffe was on 4 March, the last V2 landed in Kent on 27 March, and two days later, the last V1s fell in Ditchingfield, Hertfordshire.

By the end of the war, areas across the United Kingdom had been targeted. In addition to the cities mentioned above, bombed areas included Birmingham, West Bromwich, Bristol, Sheffield, Manchester

OVERLEAF: Art treasures being brought out of their wartime storehouse in the underground station below Piccadilly Circus, London.

Portsmouth, Southampton, Plymouth, Merseyside, Clydeside, Cardiff, Hull, Swansea, Belfast and, owing to a navigational error, Dublin. Rural locations were also vulnerable as pilots offloaded their bombs before returning home, or if their targeting was successfully led astray by British blocking devices. The German bombers, V1s, V2s and long-range guns based on the French coast had destroyed 222,000 homes and damaged nearly five million more.

The number of civilian casualties is estimated to be 60,595, and 86,000 individuals suffered serious injuries. The heaviest casualties were in 1940 and 1941, when the Blitz claimed over 20,000 deaths a year. Almost half of the civilian dead were in London, where there were 29,890 casualties. Two per cent of the fatalities were in Ireland. The comparable figures for

Germany were even higher, where the death toll in Hamburg alone equalled that in all of Britain. Nearly one million German civilians died in the Second World War.

A variety of bombs landed on UK soil. These included butterfly bombs, anti-personnel bombs which exploded when stepped on or handled; delayed actions bombs, or land mines, eight-foot bombs dropped by parachute and High Explosive (HE) bombs, usually dropped once incendiaries had created enough fires to light up the target. They often fell in sticks – a number dropping in quick succession. By the end of the Blitz, roughly 18,800 tons of HEs had landed on London, and 11,700 tons on the provinces. Planes also dropped propaganda (asking, for example, what possible defence 'armchair strategists' would have against the 'mysterious flying meteors' or V1s) or flares, providing bright lighting by which the following bombers could aim. As German pilots were encouraged to use shallow dive-bombing for greater accuracy, they were also able to machine-gun the area below. This was known as strafing (from the German *strafen*, meaning 'to punish'). Although this seldom led directly to civilian casualties, it could hamper civil defence teams trying to fight fires, and contributed to a sense of vulnerability.

The weapons of the final phase of the Blitz deserve particular mention: Hitler's secret weapons – the V1, a pilotless bomb and the V2s, powerful rockets. The 'V' came from the German *Vergeltungswaffen*, meaning weapons of retaliation and revenge. The first V1s (nicknamed 'doodle-bugs' or 'buzz bombs' because of their characteristic sound) landed in Britain on 13 June 1944, launched from sites in the Pas de Calais a week after D-Day. Most were aimed at London but some fell on surrounding areas. V1s landed when their fuel ran out, and even if shot down, would still explode. The cover of this volume shows a woman rescue worker lifting a child from the ruins of a wrecked building in Buckingham Gate, Victoria, on 23 June 1944 after a V1 attack.

V1s could be launched from the air or from the ground. It was not easy for Anti-Aircraft Command to find an effective response. It proved difficult to co-ordinate the three lines of defence, so that planes from Fighter Command risked being fired on by their own anti-aircraft defences, and AA batteries competed with Balloon Command for sites. The success rate in June 1944 was very low, between nine and thirteen

RIGHT: Scientists experimenting with a V2 rocket at Cuxhaven B.A.O.R. This picture shows the rocket standing in a vertical firing position with the elevating support slightly withdrawn.

per cent, improving only when the AA belt was largely moved down to the south coast, and gunners were equipped with the new American SCR 584 radar system. The new BTL predictor aided accuracy in gun laying and the new 'proximity fuse' shells also contributed to the rising success rate, reaching 74 per cent by the end of August. The launching pads in northern France were overrun in that month by the invading Allied forces, but V1s could still be launched from a plane.

It was even more difficult to defend against the V2s, which began arriving in August 1944. The Government did not, therefore, officially confirm that the country was being attacked by rocket until November.

LEFT: In the foreground of the photograph is the propulsion unit of a 'V' rocket bomb. March 1945.

OVERLEAF: The remains of a V2 rocket bomb being examined at Chinatown, Limehouse, London.

The rockets travelled at above 3,500 mph (five times the speed of sound), climbed to over 300,000 feet and landed almost vertically. Unlike the V1s, there was no warning provided by the delay between the engine cutting out and the subsequent explosion. As was the case with V1s, shot down over land, V2s were as lethal as those that crashed when their fuel cut out. Furthermore, the psychological impact of these weapons should not be underestimated. The attacks were unpredictable, frequently in daylight, and came after five weary years of war. A woman working in the Air Ministry told me she burnt all her diaries when the flying bombs came, certain she would not survive them. Another woman described the effectiveness of the psychological warfare of the flying bombs: 'It was horrific to hear that steady buzz, buzz, buzz. "Oh my God is it going to be us, no, it won't be us, I think it's gone over, I think it's gone, no, no. Yes, yes, it's about Ascot that. Oh Mabel, she'll get it."'

Although human losses were lower if V2s were shot down over sea or open country, the only effective defence against the rockets was to destroy them on the ground or in storage, or bomb the launching sites. By the end of the war, over five hundred V2s had landed on London, causing extensive damage and nearly 10,000 casualties. Although there were eight times as many flying bombs as there were rockets, the latter killed and injured twice as many people on average. However the British propaganda machine successfully denied the enemy the propaganda success it had been seeking. By acknowledging limited damage, the British Government was able to represent the new weapons as a nuisance rather than a significant blow, and misinformation suggested their range had been miscalculated. In the long term, the greatest significance of V1s and V2s was in the American and Soviet space programmes, and the development of inter-continental ballistic missiles.

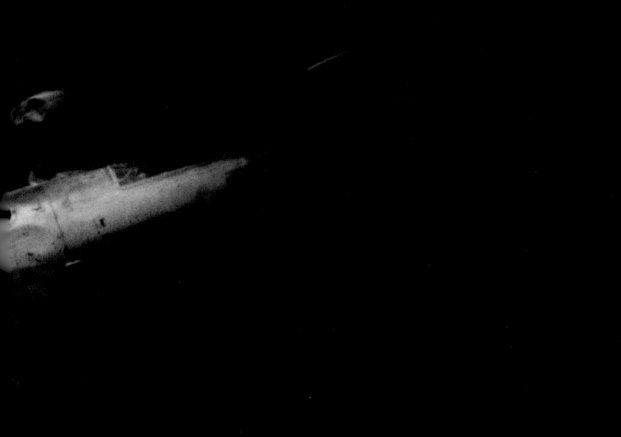

THE VI ROCKET

In 1942, Hitler gave the order to increase the rate of air attacks on Britain.

The Nazis soon developed the VI rocket, but the Allies, through bombing

raids, managed to halt production until June 1944. In only ten months, the

Germans launched 10,494 flying bombs. Travelling at a speed of 400mph with

a range of 149 miles, they were powered by a pulse engine and usually

launched via a catapult. Allied anti-aircraft fire shot many down, but 2,400 got

through and hit London, resulting in 24,165 casualties.

THE V2 ROCKET

On 8 September 1944, the Germans launched the first V2 rocket from Holland at Paris. That same night two more V2s were launched from the Ardennes and landed on the outskirts of London, one killing three people and injuring ten others.

On 12 October 1944, Hitler ordered that the V2 should be concentrated on Britain and Belgium, and during the following six months, one thousand V2s landed in Britain, half of them on London. At its peak, over one hundred V2 rockets a week were landing on the port of Antwerp.

Unlike the V1, the V2 arrived unseen, travelling at 3,500 feet per second. The development of this long-range ballistic missile has had a lasting effect on the nature of warfare.

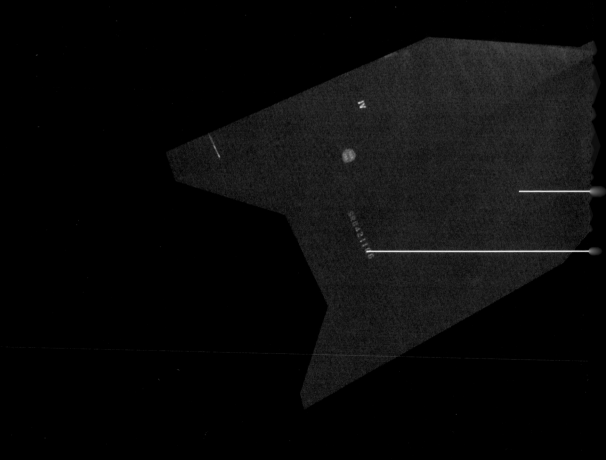

V2 TECHNICAL SPECIFICATIONS

Warhead: 2,200lb (91,00kg) of high explosive

Range: 186 miles (300 km)

Guidance: radio control or internal accelerometer, which cut off

the engine over the target, then unguided ballistic flight

Length: 47ft (14.3m)

Span: 10ft (3m)

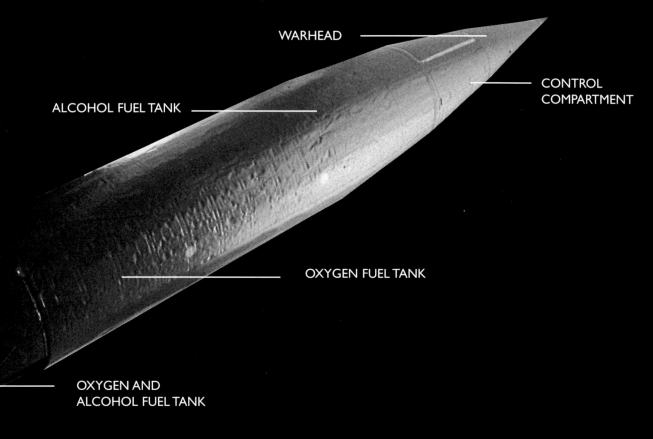

WARHEAD

CONTROL
COMPARTMENT

ALCOHOL FUEL TANK

OXYGEN FUEL TANK

OXYGEN AND
ALCOHOL FUEL TANK

COMBUSTION CHAMBER

BELOW: Seen from a Fleet Street rooftop, these pictures were the first to be released by the censor, showing a flying bomb actually crashing in central London. The distinctive skyline of London's Law Courts clearly locates the scene of the incident. Falling in a side road off the famous Drury Lane, this bomb blasted, among other buildings, the offices of the Daily Herald. Its engine cut out, the bomb plummets down behind the tower of the Law Courts.

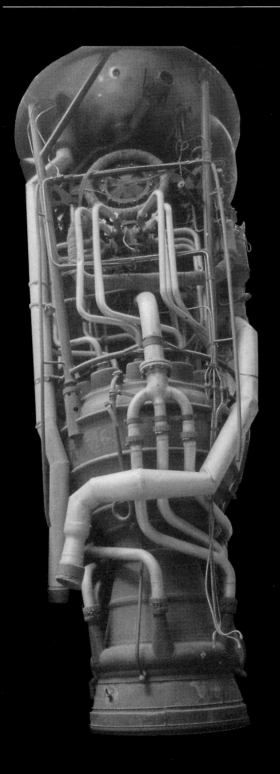

ABOVE: Engine of a V2 rocket.

LEFT: A VI rocket flies overhead during a raid.

CHAPTER 2

AIR-RAID PRECAUTIONS

THE BLITZ HAD SEVERAL GOALS: to prepare for a possible invasion of Britain, to disrupt the military and industrial machine, and to destroy civilian morale by causing widespread disruption and destruction. A variety of strategies had to be developed to meet the aerial threat to life, property and industry. The first was prophylactic: the enemy had to be prevented from reaching their target. This was the primary role of the military (anti-aircraft and balloon barrages), the night fighters, and radar.

LEFT: Making barrage balloons at the Dunlop balloon factory, Manchester.

The second was to minimise the after-effects of a raid through efficient civil defence, which involved setting up an effective system of Air Raid Precautions (ARP), and drawing in significant numbers of civilians.

This is not the place to go into depth on the role of the Royal Air Force in the air war against the Luftwaffe, but the statistics are telling: 59,223 aircrew were killed in RAF Bomber Command, in comparison to the 60,595 civilian casualties in the bombing of Britain. The defence of Britain's skies did not only take place in the air: RAF fliers were dependent on the women in Operations ('Ops') Rooms, on the crews manning the anti-aircraft guns, on the ground staff, and on the factories

RIGHT: WAAFs in an operations room.

manufacturing aeroplanes and weapons. A vast array of technology was developed to fight the air war. The battle in the air was also a battle for the most accurate radio-signalling devices to permit target location: the German *Knickebein, X-Gerät,* and *Y-Gerät,* for example, created beams to guide German pilots to their targets. They were not always successful: the first Baedeker raid on April 23-23, for example, was a failure as none of the bombers could find the target city of Exeter.

The British countered German technology with jammers, misinformation and radar. The cracking of the Enigma code, which enabled the deciphering of German codes, played a major part in British national defence. However information was not always be acted upon, to prevent arousing enemy suspicion of British possession of an Enigma machine. It should also be pointed out that even when the British did know the target, numbers, height or approach of the German bombers, until the radar system was well developed and could be complemented by a suitable night fighter, it remained very difficult to intercept them.

It was equally difficult to defend an air attack from the ground. Anti-aircraft fire was very inaccurate: figures in 1940 suggested that a hit took 2,444 rounds from heavy guns, or 1798 shells. Even these figures are likely to be low estimates. AA batteries could be equipped with either 'heavy' guns, mainly 3.7 or 4.5 inch, or 'light' guns, although other possibilities included extra-heavy 5.25 twin naval guns, and multi-barrelled rockets. Anti-aircraft (AA) batteries were 'mixed', with women responsible for the 'gun-laying' (i.e. aiming) but not permitted to fire the weapons. The Home Guard also served on the ack-ack (AA) guns.

OVERLEAF: Barrage balloons dotted the sky in an attempt to deter bombers.

RAF pilots awaiting scrambling.

Radar played an important part in the success of gun-laying and use of searchlights. The new radar-led searchlights were in position by early 1943, and 1,000mph Z battery rockets fired in AA barrage.

The skies were also defended with barrage balloons, or 'blimps', huge silver balloons tethered to steel cables. Their function was to force bombers to fly high and thereby render accurate bombing more difficult. They were first erected in London on 9 October 1938 and were gradually floated over any city likely to be a target. It is probable that the second Baedeker raid on Norwich on the night of May 8-9 was deterred because a balloon barrage had been erected. The city was also protected by the existence of a decoy site near the town. Such decoy sites called 'starfish sites' were situated near major target areas. Set alight at the start of a raid, starfish sites were intended to lure bombers away from their real target. Anti-aircraft fire, barrage balloons and decoy sites encouraged bombs to fall in more open areas, where human casualties might be lower, but where country dwellers had to cope with the subsequent destruction.

Another strand in the prophylactic approach to bombing was the black-out, introduced on 1 September 1939, in an attempt to make it difficult to passing aircraft to identify their location by city lights. It initially had a contrary effect on civilian health, with a one hundred per cent rise in casualties from road accidents in the first month. Regulations were eased a little; cars permitted masked headlights, and pedestrians pin-beam torches. The Government introduced summer time in February,

OVERLEAF: Painting cows with white stripes on an Essex farm, to make them visible to motor vehicles during the blackout.

supplemented by double summer time in the summer months. The full moon made it easier for people to find their way, but this was as true for German pilots as it was for British pedestrians. Individuals found imaginative ways of meeting the challenge of the blackout. An advertisement for blackout coats for dogs recommended that one should 'carry a white Pekinese', for example, and one enterprising farmer had his livestock protected by having white stripes painted on his dark cows. The replacement of the blackout with the 'dim-out' in September 1944 was a welcome sign of the changing fortunes of war.

LEFT: Children being evacuated from London to the countryside as troops pass.

OVERLEAF: The Women's Voluntary Services helping with evacuation. These women at a railway station are supervising a trolley fully loaded with young evacuees en route for the country.

FOLLOWING PAGE: AA Gunners on the look-out for enemy planes.

The attempts to intercept the bombers in the air, or deter them from bombing the mainland, would never be fully effective. The provisions for minimising damage on the ground and bringing rapid relief of bombed areas were therefore imperative if production and morale were not to be fatally impaired. The Government took steps to protect production and those perceived as the most vulnerable in the population through evacuation schemes. At the beginning of the war about one-and-a-half million mothers and children were evacuated from London alone. The images of crocodiles of children at train stations, sporting brown luggage labels giving their names and addresses, remains one of the most poignant images of the war. The photograph included in this collection of evacuated children passing soldiers at the station reminds us that no member of the population could avoid being part of the war effort. Despite government campaigns, however, many evacuees returned during the phoney war. Although further waves of evacuations followed the bombing in later months, they were never on the same scale. Once again, by 1942 half of the 1,340,000 people evacuated in the second government scheme had returned home. Nonetheless, as the historian Angus Calder points out, between 1939 and 1945, there were roughly sixty million changes of address in a civilian population of 38 million. War factories were relocated from cities to less vulnerable areas so workers were directed around the country. By mid-1943, London housed 76 per cent of its pre-war population and only fifty per cent of the inhabitants of the East End remained; Liverpool was reduced to eighty per cent and Southampton to sixty-seven per cent of their pre-war populations. The Blitz made a substantial contribution to this 'war of movement', as populations moved to avoid the bombing.

CHAPTER 3

AIR-RAID SHELTERS

If CIVILIAN CASUALTIES were to be kept as low as possible, the provision of air-raid shelters would be an imperative part of the war effort. Ironically, because of the predictions of high air-raid casualties prior to the war, the range of services for the dead did not come under the same strain as the services for survivors, which were utterly inadequate. As late as February 1941, one Londoner in five was 'unprotected' by any kind of officially provided shelter. The large department stores used their basements or had their own air-raid shelters. In hospitals, patients were placed on their mattresses under

LEFT: In this trench shelter which has been flooded, the shelter marshal sees that his sleepers are kept covered while he makes his rounds. Newspapers have been laid on the floor in an effort to soak up the water.

their beds. Although shelters improved as the war continued, at the beginning of the war, public shelters, or 'surface shelters' (aimed at those caught in the open when the air-raid sirens went) were often hastily erected, unsanitary at best, and poorly constructed at worst. Although the trench shelters found in parks and fields were more prone to flooding and offered little protection, they were therefore more popular than the poorly constructed brick-surface shelters. The large public shelters attracted public concern for their lack of sanitation and lighting, the Communist Party amongst the most active campaigners for better shelters. Ellen Wilkinson, MP for Jarrow, was appointed in October 1940 as Joint Parliamentary Secretary to Herbert Morrison, the Minister of Home Security, to address the problems of shelters: she was nicknamed 'Red Ellen'.

By the end of the war there were eight deep shelters (between eighty and 105 feet deep) in London which could hold eight thousand people each. Their construction had not begun until November 1940. General

Lee suggested in his diary in autumn 1940 that the delay was owing to the expense of erecting secure deep shelters. Angus Calder, the historian, suggests that a further motivation was government fears that Britain would become a nation of troglodytes opting out of the war effort.

Although government fears were never realised, in Chislehurst, Kent, a section of British society did indeed become cave dwellers. The caves consisted of several miles of passageways and larger spaces up to twenty foot square. Adapted for use as an air-raid shelter, the caves were owned by a Mr Gardiner, who had previously used them to grow mushrooms. A small entry fee was charged which was invested in improvements such as light, canteens, medical aid, cinemas, and a dance hall. By the beginning of November 1940, eight thousand women, men and children were using the caves and hundreds had to be turned away.

Although only four per cent of the public used the Tube tunnels, the shelterers in the Underground have remained one of the most enduring images of the London Blitz. In the First World War, the Tube shelters had been used by East Enders fleeing from German bombers. The platforms, however, were not officially sanctioned as shelters at first but individuals could gain access simply through buying the cheapest Tube ticket. As in the large public shelters, there were problems with facilities (the lack of lavatories and drinking water in particular). Once the authorities accepted that the use of the Tube's tunnels as air-raid shelters was not to be stopped, facilities improved. Some stations even had three-tier bunk beds so that not everyone had to spread a blanket out on the floor. Families developed a routine to secure their place, sending a child early to stake a claim, or arriving after 7.30pm when the amount of platform space was extended, although trains did not stop until 10.30pm.

The 'Tilbury' shelter in the arches and vaults under the railway at Stepney also acquired a reputation, although a less savoury one as sixteen thousand people crammed into a space which officially could hold three thousand. It was feared that amassing such large numbers of people would encourage the spread of diseases such as bronchitis and scabies. In fact, the impact of the Blitz on civilian health was not entirely as expected: rather than a massive rise in neurological disorders, Britain's mental health seemed to be improving and suicide rates fell.

An alternative to braving the perils of the public shelters was to shelter at home. There were two main types of domestic shelter: the Anderson shelter and the Morrison shelter. The Anderson shelter required fourteen corrugated-iron sheets and took four to six people, but it could only be erected by those with gardens. The Government issued advice on how to make them comfortable, but, as they were dug about three

OVERLEAF: Busy scene on a housing estate in Muswell Hill, London, when steel air-raid precaution shelters were delivered, 27 February 1938.

FOLLOWING PAGE: A Morrison shelter in use.

feet below the natural level of the garden, they often suffered drainage problems with two inches of water at the bottom. Nonetheless, some families ensured that electricity, food and drink, and family entertainments made their shelter a cosy second home.

The reluctance of individuals to go out of doors led to the introduction of the Morrison shelter in March 1941. Named after the holder of the joint office of Home Secretary and Minister for Home Security, Herbert Morrison, the shelter looked like a large steel table (large wooden kitchen tables had been shown to protect those sheltering beneath from falling masonry). It was six-foot-six inches long, four foot wide, and two-foot-nine inches high, and had a steel mattress at its base, and wire mesh sides. It usually had one tier, which could accommodate two adults and two small children (lying down). By the end of the war over one million were in use. They were offered free to those with an income under £350 per annum. Less strong than the Anderson shelter, they were nonetheless more popular.

Those families without any domestic shelters improvised. One possibility was to seek cover in the cellar, the pantry or the area under the stairs. The variety of home shelters made the work of rescuers more difficult, however. Although an Anderson shelter could withstand almost anything but a direct hit, many of the improvised shelters could not protect those who sought refuge within them. One survivor remembered the death of two children, trapped in a cellar under their bombed house. Although the room had sustained the blast, they drowned when the cellar filled with water and the window grille could not be loosened.

The Tube was not necessarily safe either. On 17 September 1940, there were twenty casualties at Marble Arch when tiles torn off by the blast became lethal missiles. On 19 November 1940, a bomb hit Sloane Square Underground Station as a train left, killing at least 79: the exact figures could not be established because many bodies could not be reconstructed. Those whose limbs were still intact were found by the rescuers with one arm up to protect their eyes. On 11 January 1941, the

roof of the booking hall at Bank Station caved in, the blast killing 38 people sheltering on the platform. When Balham Station was hit, around six hundred shelterers were killed, those surviving the blast drowning when a bomb burst a water main. Small wonder then that in early November an official census showed that only forty per cent of the population slept in a shelter, nine per cent in public shelters, four per cent in the Tube, and 27 per cent at home. As this statistic implies, the final alternative to seeking refuge in an air-raid shelter was to develop a sense of fatalism ('if a bomb has your name on it...') and refuse to interrupt normal routines.

Private rituals were invoked to offer a sense of security, and superstitions looked to for reassurance. Owners of animals might place their trust in their pet's ability to sense danger and warn the family whether they needed to take cover. Norman Longmate tells the story of a Nigerian

LEFT: An Anderson shelter in Birmingham, damaged by bomb splinters.

air-raid warden who was considered a lucky omen, and who was able to stop panic in a large air-raid shelter simply by shining a torch on his face. In the event of bombing, rational thought could save your life, or desert you entirely. Thus oral histories include tales of a Home Guard recognising in the nick of time that he needed to be in front, not behind, a wall about to be struck by a blast, or a woman refusing to lie down to avoid flying shrapnel because she might damage her stockings. A little poem by an ARP publication in Middlesborough underlined what a split-second decision could mean:

> In a raid if you must lose your head,
>
> Just remember the things that you've read.
>
> You'll know what to do;
>
> There'll only be two
>
> Kinds of people – the QUICK and the DEAD!

RIGHT: Children sleep at a neighbour's house as their own house has been bombed.

FOLLOWING PAGE: An Anderson shelter standing intact amid a scene of debris in Norwich.

LEFT: Homes have gone, lives have been lost, and there isn't a pane of glass anywhere in the street. But the parrot and his cage are absolutely intact as members of the National Fire Service carry him out of harm's way.

OVERLEAF: Taking refuge underground in Aldwych Station, 8 October 1940.

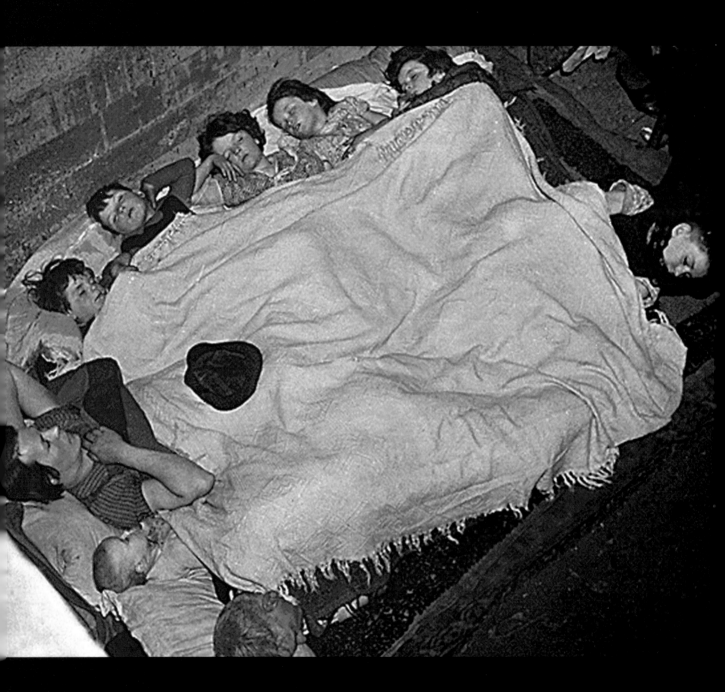

LEFT: Impromptu sleeping arrangements in London.

FOLLOWING TWO PAGES: Chislehurst Caves, in Bromley, Kent, are twelve miles from central London. The chalk caves, over twenty miles in length, date back eight thousand years.

The south east of England was hit particularly heavily by bombing, as German planes would offload unused bombs on their way home, after bombing raids on London and other cities.

These man-made caves provided the largest air-raid shelter outside London. During the spring raids of 1941, there were eight thousand people living in the caves. By the end of the year, the number was closer to fifteen thousand. At first they were officially disapproved for health and safety reasons. Eventually a cave committee was elected and the caves were run with great efficiency. The committee charged 6d a week for a family pitch. They did not have to sleep there every night to keep their pitch, but it was lost if not regularly used. No music was allowed after 9pm and the lights went out after 10.30pm. Eventually there was a cinema, water and electrical supplies, a church, telephone, bank and, as can be seen from these pictures, first-aid facilities.

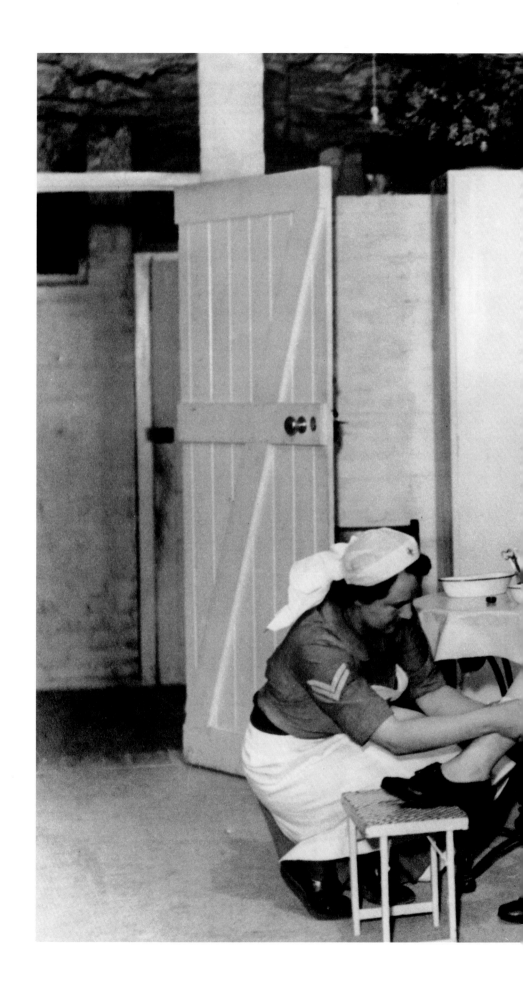

CHAPTER 4

THE HUMAN AND PHYSICAL COST OF THE WAR

CASUALTIES WERE NOT only the result of the actual explosion and the subsequent damage to housing, when people were crushed beneath rubble. Victims could be killed by the blast, the powerful wind generated by an explosion. Bodies were found in shelters apparently untouched by high explosives. Appearing to sleep, the victims had died of extreme heat or asphyxiation. Fires, burst water mains and explosions

LEFT: Rescue workers listen and try to rescue victims trapped beneath the rubble after an attack by a flying bomb in 1944.

resulting from hit gas mains contributed to the chaos following a raid. Another danger was shrapnel, the splinters of metal from exploded bombs or AA shells. Over five hundred bodies were too mangled ever to be identified. Most deaths were caused by blast, splinters or fallen masonry (and the subsequent impediments to public services). Victims could spend days trapped next to the mutilated corpses of their loved ones. Injuries could be as slight as bruising, or result in permanent disability. One woman, for example, was permanently disfigured after a raid which left her trapped under her house. Surviving the raid, the injury occurred when, in the confusion to free the survivors, the air-raid warden accidentally stood on her face.

RIGHT: Children sit waiting outside the rubble of their home.

OVERLEAF: Photograph taken after bombing of the LCC school at Ardgowan Road, London.

Children who remained in bombed areas found ways of accommodating the war, collecting shrapnel, playing in bomb craters, or 'bagging' (putting out) incendiaries with dustbin lids. However some became victims of the Blitz not through enemy action, but because they drowned in the static water tanks erected to ensure a water supply for the firefighters. Although there are few photographs of the human cost of the Blitz, a notable exception is provided by the moving photographs taken after the bombing of the London County Council school at Ardgowan Road in London. Coming to terms with loss was not aided by the sense of unreality that surrounded many Blitz victims, whose fate appeared to underline the arbitrary nature of death.

The cost of the Blitz in terms of the physical fabric of the nation is more easily explored through the visual record that remains. Each image of rubble indicates a primary goal of aerial bombardment: the de-housing of workers and the resulting decline in civilian morale. From September 1940 to May 1941, 1,150,000 houses were destroyed in London. In Coventry, nearly 50,000 houses were damaged and 20,000 rendered uninhabitable. In Clydebank, by Glasgow, all but seven of its 12,000 houses were damaged and 35,000 out of 47,000 people made homeless. In total, out of thirteen million houses in 1939, 200,000 were destroyed and 3,750,000 damaged, many of them several times. In human terms, this meant that two-and-a-quarter million people were de-housed: between 1940 and 1941, one person in six in London was rendered homeless. It is worth noting that in the period between 1934 and 1939,

OVERLEAF: A policeman, civilian and two rescue workers carry a stretcher holding a badly injured woman away from the scene of a V2 explosion in Smithfield Market, London, 9 March 1945.

245,272 houses were demolished or closed: the housing standards in Britain before the war were bad enough already. Thus it was possible for Londoners to quip that Hitler had saved the Government millions in slum clearance.

Individual families could find themselves repeatedly bombed out of their homes. One civil servant was bombed out so often that she stopped trying to find accommodation and lived in the office air-raid shelter. Others found themselves living in houses without doors, windows or ceilings. In the roads where an individual building had sustained a direct hit, the line of houses with the gap in the middle made for a peculiar sight, as Raymond Postgate described, like 'one tooth drawn out of a row.' The damage caused to houses which remained standing could be equally surreal, devastated rooms adjoining walls still sporting their paintings; facades ripped off to reveal the interior of the house like a doll's house. Rural landscapes could also be transformed. An employee of the gas company during the war, remembered how a bomb landed in a potato patch: 'It really was peculiar because there was a great hole and you could see all the potatoes, as if somebody had arranged them in a pattern.'

There were various ways in which civilians could attempt to protect their homes from all but a direct hit. Sticking tape, or even paper, on the glass could reduce the potentially lethal effects of flying glass. Leaving the front and back doors open could ease the effect of the blast tearing through a house. The populace swapped tips such as plugging ears with rimmed rubber with a string attached to prevent it being permanently stuck inside, or biting on a cork or a piece of rubber to

prevent cracked teeth or bitten tongues. No house was prepared for an air raid without buckets of sand, water, and a stirrup pump, but even these were in short supply as late as June 1942. The threat of the raids could also be met by putting together a first-aid set, storing a reserve of food, mostly tins, and clearing the attic as an anti-incendiary measure. The Government issued stern posters on the penalties for looting houses after a raid, threatening that 'looting from premises which have been damaged or vacated by reason of war operations is punishable by death or penal servitude for life.' These severe punishments were never inflicted, although looting was not uncommon, particularly in the period between the beginning of the blackout and the arrival of the first bombers.

LEFT: This building was completely destroyed after firebombs and high explosives hit the capital in April 1941.

The greatest damage to housing came not from the explosives but the incendiary bombs and fire. Ton for ton, incendiary bombs, which were usually about one foot long by two inches wide, and weighed two pounds, were nearly five times as effective at causing damage as high explosives. Incendiary bombs were often only the prelude to the main attack and were used to illuminate further targets. It was therefore imperative that they should be extinguished quickly, both to avoid the fire spreading beyond control, and to forestall the dropping of high explosive bombs on them. Civilians had to learn not to throw water on bombs, as this would cause them to explode. Sand and the stirrup pump were the most effective response, but they required manpower. Effective firefighting, therefore, was dependent on having a sufficient number of people to act swiftly and effectively to put out fires which began at empty houses and offices.

The British housing situation, unsatisfactory when the war broke out, was severely worsened by the call-up of builders, the movement of the British population, and the impact of German bombs. The emergency scheme for prefabricated houses could not resolve the problem. Although popular, only 160,000 were manufactured, rather than half a million as Churchill had promised in 1944. And although the Labour Government was elected in 1945 not least for its housing programme, pre-war rates of construction would not be reached. In 1951, the housing shortage was still estimated at between one and two million.

OVERLEAF: Damage caused in March 1945 by V2 rocket at the junction of Wanstead Park Road and Endsleigh Gardens, Ilford. Nine people were killed, and 15 seriously injured. Eight houses were destroyed, 16 had to be demolished, 33 were made uninhabitable and 116 were very seriously damaged.

FOLLOWING PAGE: Ministry of Works Emergency Prefabricated House, 1945. Designed by the Aircraft Industries and made from aluminium because its light weight for transport and handling.

ABOVE: Coventry after a raid, 14 November 1940.

LEFT: First-aid repairs being carried out on No 10 Downing Street.

OVERLEAF: Royal Welsh Fusiliers help clear up after damage after heavy bombing in Belfast, 7 May 1941.

CHAPTER 5

CIVIL DEFENCE

A BROAD RANGE of organisations were involved in the Blitz: air-raid wardens, controllers (each district had a control centre, to which the wardens reported), firefighters, bomb disposal (BD) squads who dealt with unexploded bombs (UXB), individuals manning the First Aid Posts (FAP), Messenger Services, the Salvation Army, Home Guards, the National Fire Service (NFS) and the Women's Voluntary Service (WVS). Plane-spotters were trained to recognise each German plane by its

LEFT: Guarding stock salvaged from a grocer's shop after an air raid on Birkenhead, March 1941.

silhouette and the sound of its engines. 'Jim Crows', as observers were called, were organised to reduce the impact of air raids, particularly on wartime production. Individuals could remain at work despite the sirens until the spotters sounded the 'crash warning', a series of staccato blasts on klaxon horns when bombers were not merely in the vicinity but coming close. The Emergency Medical Services (EMS), originally intended for servicemen, expanded to include blitz victims. A further consequence of the air raids was the unified Emergency Hospital Scheme (EHS), a reorganisation of the medical services to permit an

LEFT: Warden on the roof of a building on look-out for enemy planes flying over London. St Paul's Cathedral is clearly visible in the background, the surrounding area as yet undamaged by the massive bombardments that flattened the area later in the war.

OVERLEAF: Searching for flying bombs.

efficient response to air-raid casualties. These provided a basis for the National Health Service after the war.

Even before the war, the Government realised that the Home Front would require defence over and above that offered by the Armed Forces. In 1937, the Air Raid Precautions (ARP) Act had made it compulsory for local authorities, of whom there were 250, to set up Civil Defence Organisations. These were divided into specialised sections including Rescue, First Aid, Ambulance, Communications and Decontamination (poison gas). Civil Defence was based on the idea that each neighbourhood would be in the best position to help itself. From 1939 to 1946, direct civil defence on the home front cost £1,026,561,000.

OVERLEAF: Civil defence outside Belfast.

Nonetheless, only a fifth of the Civil Defence's million and a quarter workers were full-time paid workers. In the early months of the war over one-and-a-half million men and women were enrolled in Civil Defence, rising to two million as the war continued. They were not treated equally: women had to fight for protective clothing and their right for equal compensation under the Personal Injuries (Emergency Provisions) Act, which was not granted until 1943.

In the period of the phoney war, full-time ARP workers, of whom there were 400,000, were criticised for having cushy jobs. Air-raid wardens, whose responsibilities included patrolling the streets to ensure no chink of light penetrated the blackout, could easily be perceived as self-important busybodies. However when the raids came, the wardens' local knowledge could make the difference between life or death.

In January 1941, the Government launched a Fire Guard scheme which made it compulsory for there to be a guard on duty in buildings in those areas where attack was considered likely. The Fire Guard was distinguished by an armlet and a pudding-basin steel helmet. They were armed with a stirrup pump. The original call had conscripted men aged sixteen to sixty, but the scheme was first extended to include women between the ages of twenty and forty-five in August 1942, and then men up to 63, and individuals outside those age groups were encouraged to volunteer. The last fire-watchers were disbanded on 2 May 1945.

Although the scheme theoretically resulted in an army of fire-watchers numbering over six million, in practice it was relatively easy to attain an exemption and not every individual listed on the fire rota actually turned up. Tiring and unpopular, like so many of the civil defence duties, fire-watching was a serious burden to bear for those already working the long hours of a full-time job. Furthermore, guarding an empty office or factory was more unpleasant than being on duty in one's own street. Nonetheless, in the Baedeker raid on Canterbury, when six thousand incendiaries were dropped, 75 per cent were put out by fire-watchers without help from the NFS. One reason why St Paul's Cathedral survived the sea of flames in the London Blitz was because it had a large and committed band of fire-watchers. Other areas were less lucky. Unattended fires were a particular problem in those areas where a new phenomenon was becoming established, 'trekking'. In the provincial raids, it was observed that individuals were leaving the cities as darkness approached to spend the night up to thirty miles away from the target area, and returning in the morning. In 1941, for example, up to one hundred thousand people trekked to sleep outside Belfast.

Firefighting was also not aided by the fact that there were over 1,500 fire authorities. Relations between the Fire Brigade and the Auxiliary Fire Service (AFS) were not always cordial, and co-operation between localities was complicated by the discovery that equipment was frequently incompatible. In consequence, in August 1941 the National Fire Service was created, reorganising the different brigades (and AFS) into around forty 'fire forces' under central control. Further firefighting measures included the provision of tanks and pipes to provide emergency water supplies. Technology and nature could combine to make the post-raid operations even more complicated than they already were. In the raid on Bristol on 3 January 1941, it was so cold that the uniforms of the firefighters froze as they attempted to bring the blazes

RIGHT: A typical searchlight, now on display in London's Imperial War Museum.

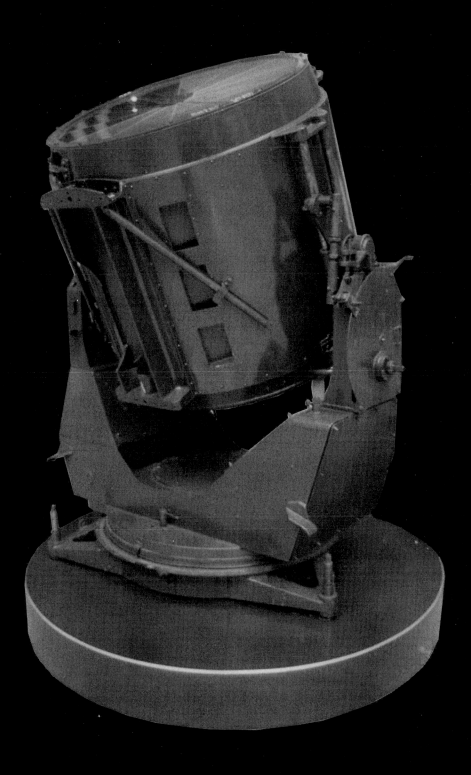

under control. The casualty rates of firefighters serve as a reminder of their dedication: 793 firemen and 25 fire-women lost their lives in the war, and seven thousand were seriously injured, many blinded.

The high number of injured and bombed-out individuals caused public concern for the inadequate aid available for the victims of air raids. The experience of Coventry showed that however good the system for the immediate consequences of raids (fire, gas escapes, debris and so on), it was the homeless who determined the morale of the area. The Government had prepared for high casualties, but it had put less thought into the assistance which the bombed-out would require. Government provision for those without fuel, light, hot food, drinking water and rest remained inadequate, and many times affected areas did not have the information or guidance that would permit an effective response. The bureaucracy of war rendered a difficult situation more so. In London alone there were 96 authorities to whom the bombed-out could turn. The spirit of the Poor Law still determined official responses, so that local authorities, for example, were supposed to distinguish between their own 'native' homeless and those from another locality, even if that locality was only a street away. Rationing and registration created another layer of problems, as individuals trudged around numerous government offices attempting to replace their papers. By February 1941 Malcolm Macdonald, the Minister of Health, had promised Treasury backing to any measures the local authorities in the United Kingdom considered necessary. There remained great regional differences in defences and 'post-raid services'. Belfast, for example, which was not raided until April 1941, had no search lights, few ack-ack guns and had fewer shelters (which were in poor condition) than anywhere else in the United Kingdom. In the

exploratory raid of April 7, two of the German planes were able to turn on their navigation lights over the city. The raids on Belfast cost 745 lives.

The targeting of civilians created new waves of refugees, often with no obvious refuge to which to go. Provision had to be made to meet the needs of the bombed-out, from accommodation to the most basic needs, such as sustenance and clothing. Intended only as clearing houses, 'rest centres' in fact sometimes housed people for up to ten days or more, with little more to offer than cups of tea and bully-beef sandwiches. However, rest centres were not immune from attack

LEFT: A warden takes charge of a rescued child after a pilot-less plane crashed on a house in southern England, 23 June 1944.

themselves: according to Mass Observation, out of fifteen rest centres in Coventry, thirteen were hit or damaged. After these raids, rest centres were more numerous, improved and equipped. A new plan called 'Come Right In' was instigated in which registered households signalled their willingness to take in bombed-out neighbours.

Other organisations were also set up in an attempt to assist the victims of air raids with the practical aspects of life. The National Emergency Washing Service, for example, was a service sponsored by Lever Brothers for bombed-out women in rest centres. It was not only the bombed-out who had to find a way of surviving. Those individuals made homeless by unexploded bombs had no right to official assistance, and even those households who could remain in their place of residence could find themselves without windows, water, gas or electricity after a raid, and their possessions covered in splinters of glass, masonry and soot. Some areas benefited from mobile canteens and buffets, named 'blitz dives', which provided sustenance to victims and civil defence alike.

One factor which hampered civil defence, however, was the range of schemes and organisations, as each local authority was responsible for assessing the local situation. There could be clashes of competencies: the police force had separate headquarters, the ARP controller had no say over the Fire Brigade, and the Auxiliary Fire Service (AFS) was initially not incorporated into the civil defence system. The range of schemes also made it more difficult for experience to be pooled. As effective communication and accurate information played the most important role in permitting recovery, these were serious flaws. Rapid and effective response was also made more difficult by the range of Ministries responsible for the different consequences of air raids: the injured and dead, and water and sewer repairs, for example, were the responsibility of the Ministry of Heath; the Ministry of Food was responsible for the hungry; the Ministry of Home Security for salvaging furniture and clearing debris and the Ministry for Home Security and Transport for road repairs.

The restricted number of personnel who could be shared out among the Civil Defence organisations was another problem, especially given that CD duties often had to be combined with long working hours. In Canterbury, for example, the Fire Guard and the Home Guard competed for their members, reflecting a lack of manpower. This issue was not aided by unplanned evacuation and trekking, nor by local resistance to the enrolment of women in civil defence duties. Nonetheless, by 1943, one in four CD workers were female and by 1944 there were 179,800 women in civil defence, almost all in unpaid work.

The historian Raynes Minns lists some of the duties in which they were

involved: working as air-raid wardens, as shown on the cover of this

collection, fire-guard duty personnel, emergency messengers and staff at

the emergency control centres, in auxiliary medical services, at first-aid

posts, in shelters and rest centres, driving ambulances and helping

rescue parties. The Women's Voluntary Service also played a significant

role. Founded in 1938 by Lady Reading, the WVS, or 'women in

green', had half a million members by early 1940. They provided meals

and drinks after raids, (co-operating with the Ministry of Food) and

were involved as well in the auxiliary welfare services, such as those

providing clothes for the bombed-out. Although exhausting, service in

these organisations helped to sustain morale, by ensuring that

individuals felt they had a useful role to play in a collective response to

the enemy.

CHAPTER 6

MORALE

At the outset of the war, public entertainments were closed in order to prevent large numbers of individuals being killed. However, the cinemas, theatres, sports grounds and meetings reopened in December 1939, when the Government realised that their contribution to morale was more important than their vulnerability to attack. High spirits in bombed-out areas and air-raid shelters were encouraged through visits of figures as diverse as the Lancashire comic George Formby,

LEFT AND FOLLOWING PAGE: Prime Minister Winston Churchill visiting a demonstration of anti-aircraft defences.

members of the Royal Family, and Winston Churchill, who would walk unannounced through the worst affected areas, calling out such encouragements as 'Are we downhearted?'

The Blitz was not least a propaganda battle. It is not surprising, therefore, that home propaganda emphasised the courage, resolution and humour of the British. Of the capital, propagandists said 'London can take it!' Bombed-out businesses erected cheerful signs reading, for example, 'more open than usual', 'broken glass but not broken hearts' 'Blast!' and 'Gone with the Wind'. Stories of resolution and courage had great propaganda value, and personal experiences of bombing could be

OVERLEAF: George Formby entertaining Londoners sheltering in Aldwych Tube Station, November 1940.

shared, encouraging the sense of wartime community. The publican Billy Burke in Coventry described his experience, for example: 'I was about to open my pub front door when the bomb dropped. The blast, it blew me back from the door, lifted me over the counter of the bar, and I was in position ready to pour the beer!' Raymond Postgate described how one enterprising individual in London did rather well for the Spitfire fund by putting up a notice: 'If you give 6d to this fund I will let you talk about your bomb.'

Both V1s and V2s attracted similar puns and jokes reflecting gallows humour. The V1s were labelled 'Bob Hopes' – as in 'Bob down and Hope for the best'. One soldier remembers getting into a taxi in London, hesitating to listen to an ominous sound. The taxi driver

assuaged his fears: 'Oh you're all right, hop in, mate. It's a motorbike. I thought it was one of them clockwork sparrows.' One Kent farmer found a positive response to a V2 falling on his orchard in September 1944, describing it as 'the quickest apple harvest ever'.

There began to be talk of the traditional British reserve crumbling, of strangers chatting on buses, or inviting passers-by into their shelters. Characteristics associated with the 'spirit of the Blitz' included such diverse responses as improvisation (such as hitch-hiking to work when public transport was disrupted), mobile telegram boys, and group singalongs. Films like Humphrey Jennings' 'Fires were Started' (1943)

OVERLEAF: A message epitomising the 'carry-on' spirit during the Blitz, posted up behind a fruit stall in East London, or added by an imaginative editor.

helped to make heroes of civilians contributing their part to the war effort, but film of the Blitz is rare, not least because film technology in the Forties did not permit events to be filmed spontaneously and synchronously.

In contrast to the apparent drama of the Blitz, the raids could also be immeasurably tedious. Waiting for the all-clear could be a boring and uncomfortable business. Disruptions to public transport could render the journey home or to work a long and weary one. One side effect of a bombing raid was dirt, as the blast propelled huge amounts of dust and debris into the air. Furthermore, in periods of steady raids, people could go for protracted periods when they could neither change their clothes nor wash. Any activity could suddenly be interrupted (particularly problematic for some tasks, such as cooking, bathing, or going to the

lavatory). Loss of sleep was the worst problem for many. Even sleeping in the public air-raid shelters could be a challenge in itself, given the number of individuals with disruptive habits such as snoring or talking, or seeking to encourage communal singalongs. Government reports on morale showed that the German raids were having more effect than the media would ever admit.

Nonetheless, the sense of community forged by shared danger remains an important component of the memories of the survivors of the Second World War. The historian Arthur Marwick draws attention to the distinction between 'active' and passive' morale, the first involving heroic gestures, the second, a stoic willingness to continue. He links these to the transient and durable effects of the raids, from loss of sleep to the destruction of railway bridges, telephone exchanges and water and gas mains. The evidence indicates that morale was best when

162

Londoners amuse themselves underground as an impromptu performance in a shelter is given by boys playing mouth organs.

adjustment routines could be developed: in some ways, regular raids were therefore easier to cope with than unpredictable ones. When the bombers switched to smaller places and erratic patterns of attack, their goal to disrupt civilian morale was more successful. The 'hit-and-run' raids were therefore a particular blow to production and generated a general war weariness.

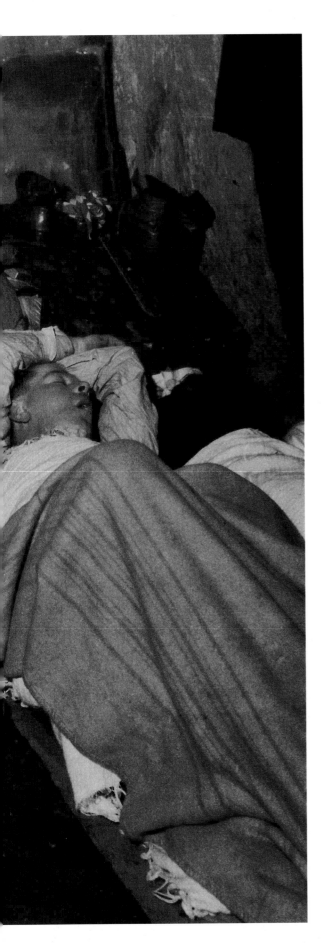

LEFT: A family sleeps in the Tube tunnel: even the girl's doll has its own improvised bed. Liverpool Street Station shelter, 12 November 1940.

OVERLEAF: A Sikh family shelters in an alcove of the crypt, Christ Church, Spitalfields, London, 6 November 1940. This photograph and the one opposite were taken by renowned photographer, Bill Brandt.

LEFT: A Woman's Voluntary Services (WVS) mobile canteen, serving rescue workers after the fall of a bomb.

OVERLEAF: Shortly after flying bomb damage to suburban houses in Norbury, London, July 1944, a picnic lunch is served from a 'Queen's messenger' funded by the American Committee for Air Raid Relief.

The Blitz was successfully constructed as an experience which affected all: young and old, rich and poor, whatever their colour or gender. The photo of the Sikh family who have sought shelter in an alcove at Christ Church, Spitalfields is an example of the photographer Bill Brandt's work, and offers a rare illustration of ethnic diversity in the Blitz. The presence of multi-ethnic residents in the East End was not always handled with sensitivity by the media at the time. Nonetheless, the construction of the Blitz as impacting on all colours, creeds and classes was an important component of the battle for morale and the emphasis on wartime camaraderie. Areas of high population and accommodation density, such as the East End of London, were clearly more vulnerable to attack than the West End. Furthermore, many working-class areas had inadequate water supplies, exacerbating the effects of the raids. Wealth could determine the comfort of the air-raid shelter, and subtle indicators of class could even be found on Anderson shelters – whether the entrances were hung over with sacking, or carpeting, for example. When Buckingham Palace was first bombed on 13 September 1940, however, it appeared to show that nobody, however privileged they might appear to be, was excluded from the Blitz. Queen Elizabeth purportedly said 'I'm glad we've been bombed. It makes me feel I can look the East End in the face.' The commitment of the Royal Family to remain in London underlined the wartime sense of 'all being in it together'.

OVERLEAF: The Royal Family travelled all over the Britain and Northern Ireland. Here HRH George is inspecting coastal defences on the Northumbrian coast, 19 July, 1940.

CONCLUSION

THE BOMBING OF the homeland epitomizes the personal experience of 'total war', in which belligerent countries experience destruction on a vast scale, the distinction between the soldier and the civilian breaks down, and the front line is everywhere. The Blitz had its own sounds: the ululating wail of the 'alert' air-raid warning, the two-minute blast of the 'all-clear', the unco-ordinated engines of the enemy aircraft, the hammering of anti-aircraft artillery, and the sudden absence of sound

LEFT: Barbed wire defences in front of the distinctive clock tower Big Ben. The Houses of Parliament were also damaged in the severest bombing raid on London. On 10 May 1941, the debating chamber of the House of Commons was ruined. MPs moved to the House of Lords to continue business as usual, and a secret submarine factory was set up beneath the bombed chamber in the 'Guy Fawkes' cellar.

when the engine of the V1 cut out. Some bombs and aircraft engines were even fitted with whistles or sirens to exploit the psychological pressure of sound. The Blitz also had its own taste and smell – a combination of masonry dust, earth, gas, fires, charred wood and flesh, and sulphur fumes. It had its own colours and lights: the artificial light indoors and the eerie darkness outside as Britain blacked out its windows, the intense beams of the searchlights, the glare of flares, and the blazing orange and pink skies after a raid.

For those who did not experience the Blitz, these sensations can only be imagined, recreated by documentary and visual evidence. Documentary

RIGHT: Railway attacked in London. Despite the impression of this image, the trains were fairly unaffected and continued to carry people across Britain.

evidence is relatively widely available, although many documents were destroyed as individuals and institutions got rid of paper records stored in attics vulnerable to incendiary bombs. The experiences on the home front are nonetheless well represented in private and public memory, in official source materials and in literary sources, from Louis McNiece's or TS Eliot's poetry, to novels by Virginia Woolf and Evelyn Waugh.

Photographic stock was in short supply in the Second World War. Many of these images therefore stem from official sources. For example, in November 1940, the Ministry of Information commissioned the photo-journalist Bill Brandt (born in Germany) to take photographs of the shelterers. In a collection of wartime images, it is worth drawing attention to the bravery of these wartime photographers. Published

LEFT: London shortly after an attack.

photographs were unlikely to challenge the construction of 'Britain can take it', an image constructed by wartime photographers such as Brandt, or Bert Hardy, whose work for the Picture Post underlined the stoicism and resilience of the British under attack. A visual record of the air war has also been passed down to us by wartime artists: Paul Nash was influenced by the topography of air war, John Piper by the evocative lines of blitzed ruins, Henry Moore was inspired by the London Tube shelterers, and Edward Burra and Francis Bacon represented the violent and destructive face of war. However, the image which has become most symbolic of the Blitz remains a photograph of 29 December 1940. It shows the dome of St Paul's rising unscathed from the smoke. It promised that the British, like their Cathedral, would endure.

St Paul's, 29 December 1940.

FURTHER READING

Angus Calder, *The People's War: Britain 1939-1945* London: Pimlico, 2000

E. R. Chamberlain, *Life in Wartime Britain London:* B. T. Batsford Ltd, 1972

Arthur Marwick, photographic research by Harold Chapman, *The Home Front. The British and the Second World War London:* Thames and Hudson. 1976

Norman Longmate, *How We Lived Then: A History of Everyday Life during the Second World War London:* Hutchinson & Co., 1971

Jane Waller and Michael Vaughan-Rees, *Blitz: The Civilian War 1940-45* London: Macdonald & Co. Ltd., 1990

Susan Briggs, *Keep Smiling Through London:* Weidenfeld & Nicolson, 1975

Personal interviews were conducted by the author working on 'The Gendering of British National Defence 1939-45', Leverhulme Research Project F/185/AK, Lancaster University 1999-2000

PICTURE ACKNOWLEDGEMENTS

Imperial War Museum: Page 6: fl146613, 10: ho1, 14: h5603, 16: h6324, 20: hu36188, 24: d3938, 25: d3940, 26: cl627, 32: hu36134, 37: bu10769, 38: bu11149, 40: hu 44937, 48: hu636, 54: hu36241, 62: ch13806, 66: hu36167, 70: hu717, 72: h39407, 76: d1555, 82: hu36151, 84: d2055, 88:d4141, 91: d24235, 92: hu36196, 94; d21220, 96: hu44272, 104: d21238, 108: hu36161, 112: hu65896, 120: ch15238, 122: mw53, 124: h36083, 125: h5597, 126: h9464, 128: h8143, 132: ch11775, 136: 17863, 144 hu 36227 150: h339498, 152: h39490, 156: hu36154, 160: hu671, 164: d1582, 166: d1516, 168: hu687, 170: hu4948, 174: h3270.

All other pictures courtesy; Chislehurst Caves, Illustrated London News, US National Archives and specially commissioned by the publisher.

184

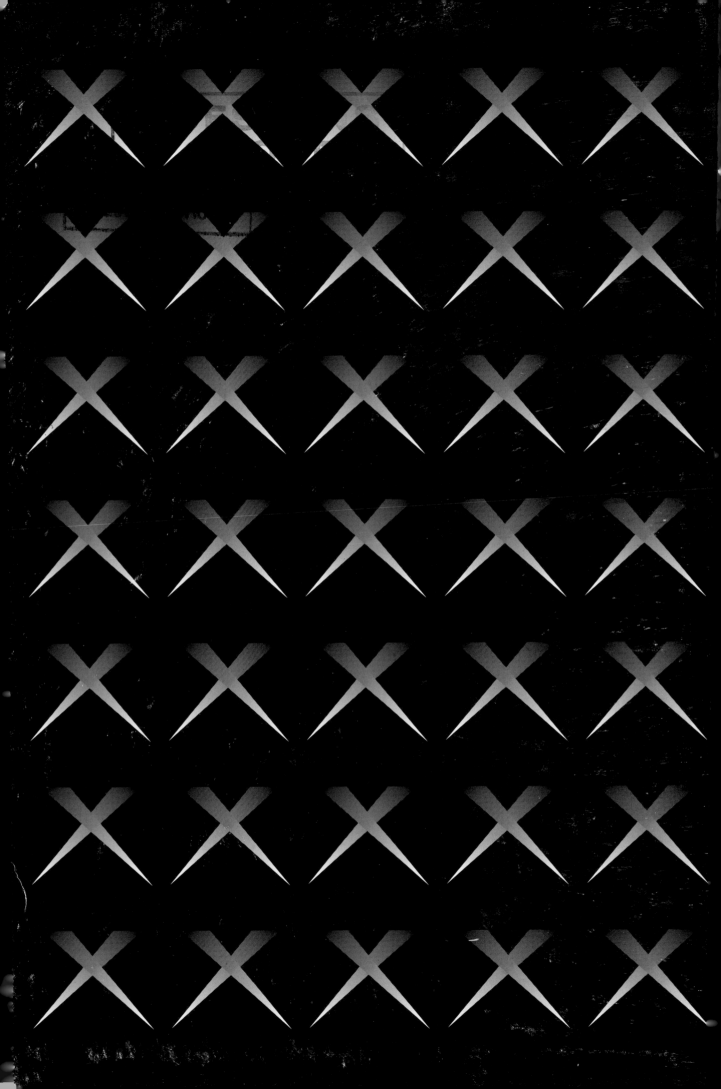